VICKI COBB
SCIENCE PLAY

I See Myself

by Vicki Cobb

illustrated by Julia Gorton

HarperCollins*Publishers*

For Jonathan Jensen Cobb
—V.C.

For Ivy, Raleigh, and Russell
—J.G.

The author gratefully acknowledges Dr. Myra Zarnowsky of Queens College for her help
in making this developmentally appropriate and Dr. David Kessler and
Dr. Sujatha Ramunujan of the Eastman Kodak Company for their technical expertise.
However, she takes full responsibility for the accuracy of the text.
She also extends a special thank-you to Andrea Curley for her brilliant editing.

Library of Congress Cataloging-in-Publication Data
Cobb, Vicki.
I see myself / by Vicki Cobb ; illustrated
by Julia Gorton.
p.   cm.
ISBN 0-688-17836-7 — ISBN 0-688-17837-5 (lib. bdg.)
1. Reflection (Optics)—Juvenile literature.
[1. Reflection (Optics) 2. Mirrors.]
I. Gorton, Julia, ill. II. Title.
QC425.2 .C63 2002   00-057220
535'.323—dc21   CIP
                                                       AC

Typography by Julia Gorton
19 SCP 21

Note to the Reader

This book is designed so that your child can make discoveries. It poses a series of questions that can be answered by doing activities that temporarily take the child away from the book. The best way to use this book is to do the activities, without rushing, as they come up during your reading. Turn the page to the next part of the text only after the child has made the discovery. That way, the book will reinforce what the child has found out through experience. Before you begin reading this book to your child, have on hand a small mirror, a flashlight, and a ball.

Look in the mirror.

Who do you see?

Your very own self,
that's who!
Now suppose there
were no mirrors
in the world.
What could you do
to see yourself?

Look at the glass in a picture frame.

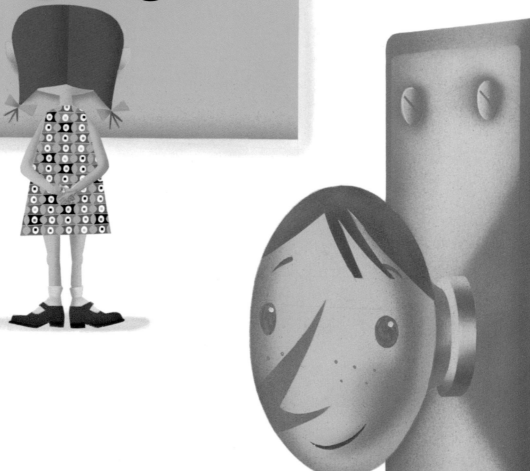

A shiny doorknob makes your face look **fat.**

How about the door of a shiny red car

or a
puddle
on the street?

Keep looking everywhere you go.
Can you see **yourself** in your mom's sweater?
Or on a page in this book?
Or in the grass?

You can see the **sweater**

and the page

and the grass.

But you can't see yourself.

You see yourself
only in shiny things.
A mirror is the shiniest
and the best thing
for seeing yourself.

But you need something besides a mirror
to see yourself. Know what it is?
Here's a hint.
Take a mirror into a closet
and close the door.

Can
you see
yourself
in the
dark?

In order to see yourself,
in order to see anything, you must have

light.

There are lots of kinds of light. There's

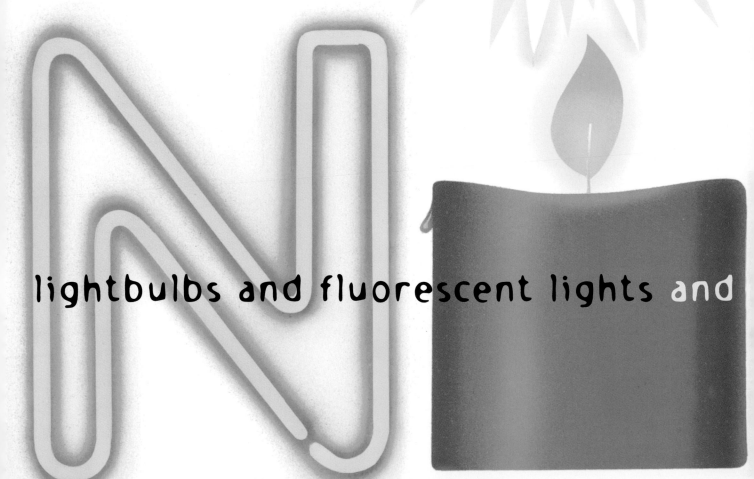

lightbulbs and fluorescent lights and

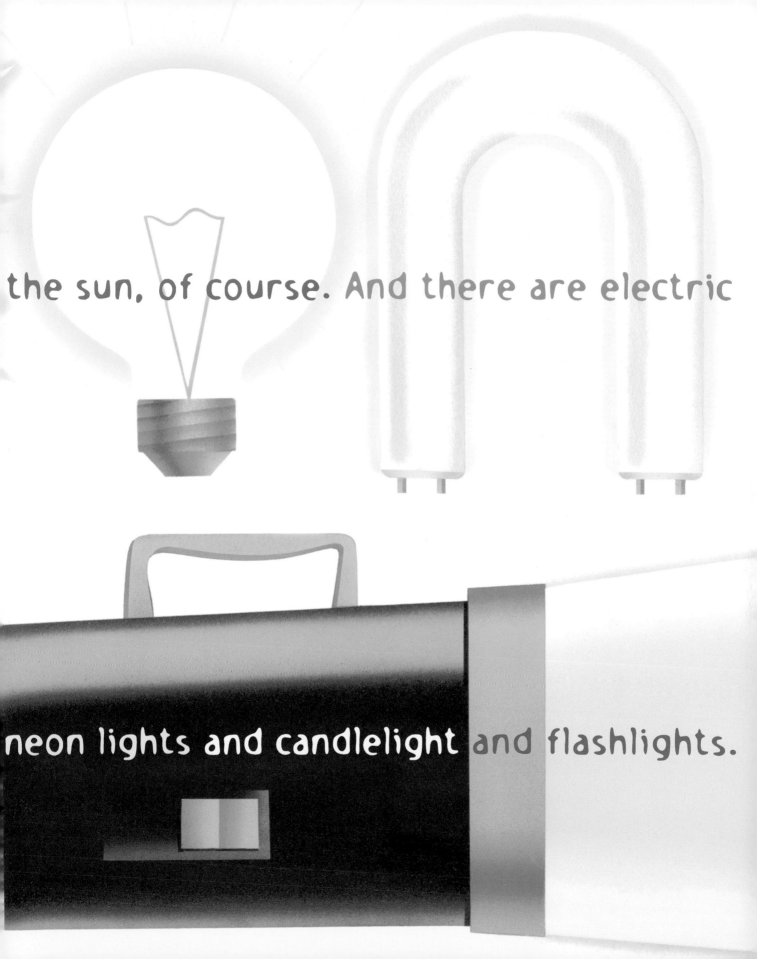

the sun, of course. And there are electric

neon lights and candlelight and flashlights.

If you  looked at yourself

in a mirror in all these lights, could you see yourself?

You bet!

How does a mirror work?

Mirrors catch light and bounce it someplace else.

Take a small hand mirror and a flashlight.

Shine the light on the mirror. See where you can send the bounced light.

Can you light up the wall? Can you light up a picture on the wall?

You can't see
light bounce.
You have to imagine
how it bounces.
Let's say a ray of light
is like a ball.
Go bounce a ball
on a smooth hard floor.
If you throw the ball
straight down,
it bounces right
back up to you.
If you throw it
on a slant,
it bounces away at
the same slant.
When you bounce
a ball on a smooth
floor, it bounces
perfectly.

What happens
if you bounce
a ball in
your room

with
toys
all
over
the
floor?

You can never tell where it will bounce.

If you threw
a bunch of
Ping-Pong balls down
in your messy room, they

would scatter,

bouncing in all directions.

A mirror is like a smooth floor for light. When a ray of light strikes a mirror, it makes a perfect bounce. A mirror handles a gazillion rays of light at once. And every one makes a perfect bounce every time.

Light doesn't only bounce off mirrors. It bounces off every object you see. When light rays bounce off this page or your mom's sweater, they scatter in many different directions. Some of the scattered light reaches your eyes. That's why you can see this page or your mom's sweater.

Scattered light bounces off your face too.

When it bounces into your mom's eyes,

she can see you, but she can't see herself.

Your face is not a mirror.

However,

when scattered light

from your face

hits a mirror,

it bounces perfectly

from the mirror

right into your eyes.

That's why you see yourself.

Yay!

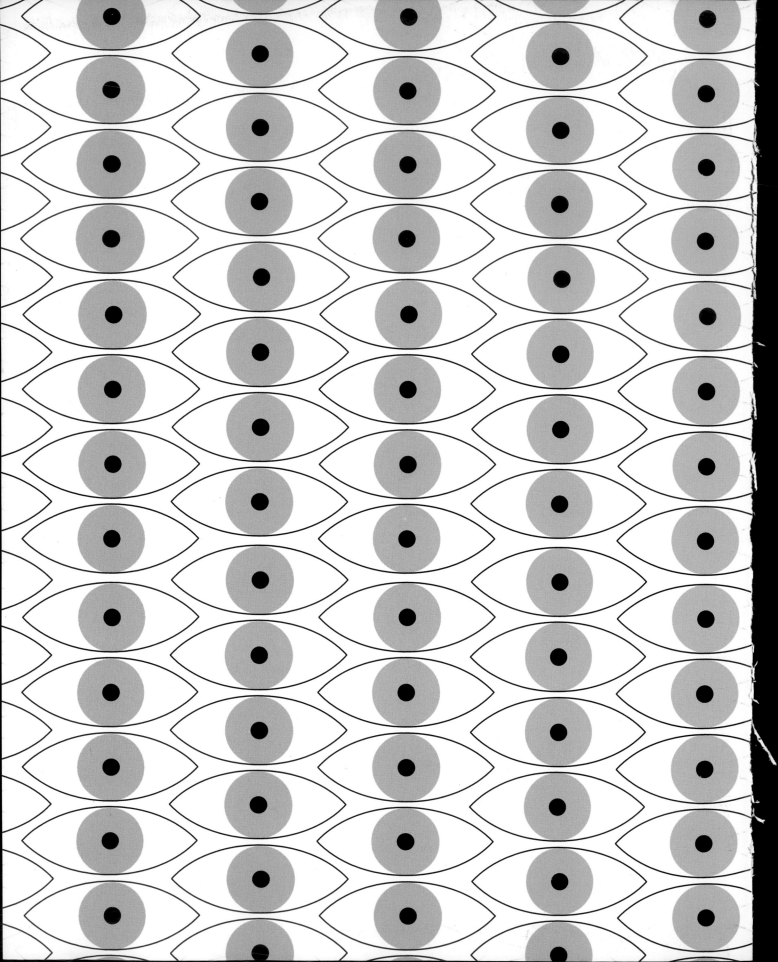